Immigration to the United States

Italian Immigrants

Michael Burgan

Robert Asher, Ph.D., General Editor

Facts On File, Inc.

Immigration to the United States: Italian Immigrants

Facts On File, Inc.
132 West 31st Street
New York NY 10001

Library of Congress Cataloging-in-Publication Data

Burgan, Michael.
   Italian immigrants / Michael Burgan.
      p. cm. – (Immigration to the United States)
   Includes bibliographical references and index.
   ISBN 0-8160-5681-1
   1. Italian Americans–History–Juvenile literature. 2. Immigrants–United States–
History–Juvenile literature. 3. Italian Americans–Juvenile literature.
   I. Title. II. Series.
   E184.I8B96 2005
   304.8'73045–dc22

                                                                                2004014303

Cover design by Cathy Rincon
A Creative Media Applications Production
Interior design: Fabia Wargin & Luís Leon
Editor: Laura Walsh
Copy editor: Laurie Lieb
Proofreader: Tania Bissell
Photo researcher: Jennifer Bright

Photo Credits:
p. 1 © Bettmann/CORBIS; p. 4 © Bettmann/CORBIS; p. 11 © CORBIS; p. 13 © Bettmann/CORBIS; p. 16 © Bettmann/CORBIS; p. 22 © Getty Images/Hulton Archive; p. 24 © Getty Images/Hulton Archive; p. 27 © Getty Images/Hulton Archive; p. 30 © Hulton-Deutsch Collection/CORBIS; p. 34 © CORBIS; p. 36 © Michael Maslan Historic Photographs/CORBIS; p. 38 © Library of Congress; p. 41 © Getty Images/Hulton Archive; p. 44 © CORBIS; p. 50 © Bettmann/CORBIS; p. 55 © Bettmann/CORBIS; p. 58 © AP Photo/Stanford University; p. 61 © Getty Images/Hulton Archive; p. 65 © AP Photo; p. 67 © AP Photo; p. 68 © AP Photo; p. 72 © AP Photo/Susan Walsh; p. 74 © AP Photo/Nick Ut; p. 75 © AP Photo; p. 79 © Getty Images/Hulton Archive; p. 81 © Ted Spiegel/CORBIS; p. 85 © AP Photo/Kathy Willens; p. 88 © AP Photo/Mike Segar

Printed in the United States of America

VH PKG 10 9 8 7 6 5 4 3 2 1

This book is printed on acid-free paper.

Previous page: Italian-American girls carry a shrine to Saint Rocco in an Italian parade during a festival in New York City in 1933.

Contents

A Nation of Immigrants

Robert Asher, Ph.D.

Left:
A group of Italian immigrant miners stand in front of their tent home in Trinidad, Colorado in 1914. Italian immigrants often found work in mining and other jobs requiring hard, physical labor during the 18th and 19th centuries.

Human beings have always moved from one place to another. Sometimes they have sought territory with more food or better economic conditions. Sometimes they have moved to escape poverty or been forced to flee from invaders who have taken over their territory. When people leave one country or region to settle in another, their movement is called emigration. When people come into a new country or region to settle, it is called immigration. The new arrivals are called immigrants.

People move from their home country to settle in a new land for two underlying reasons. The first reason is that negative conditions in their native land push them to leave. These are called "push factors." People are pushed to emigrate from their native land or region by such things as poverty, religious persecution, or political oppression.

The second reason that people emigrate is that positive conditions in the new country pull them to the new land. These are called "pull factors." People immigrate to new countries seeking opportunities that do not exist in their native country. Push and pull factors often work together. People leave poor conditions in one country seeking better conditions in another.

Sometimes people are forced to flee their homeland because of extreme hardship, war, or oppression. These immigrants to new lands are called refugees. During times of war or famine, large groups of refugees may immigrate to new countries in search of better conditions. Refugees have been on the move from the earliest recorded history. Even today, groups of refugees are forced to move from one country to another.

Pulled to America

F or hundreds of years, people have been pulled to America seeking freedom and economic opportunity. America has always been a land of immigrants. The original settlers of America emigrated from Asia thousands of years ago. These first Americans were probably following animal herds in search of better hunting grounds. They migrated to America across a land bridge that connected the west coast of North America with Asia. As time passed, they spread throughout North and South America and established complex societies and cultures.

Beginning in the 1500s, a new group of immigrants came to America from Europe. The first European immigrants to America were volunteer sailors and soldiers who were promised rewards for their labor. Once settlements were established, small numbers of immigrants from Spain, Portugal, France, Holland, and England began to arrive. Some were rich, but most were poor. Most of these emigrants had to pay for the expensive ocean voyage from Europe to the Western Hemisphere by promising to work for four to seven years. They were called indentured servants. These emigrants were pushed out of Europe by religious persecution, high land prices, and poverty. They were pulled to America by reports of cheap, fertile land and by the promise of more religious freedom than they had in their homelands.

Many immigrants who arrived in America, however, did not come by choice. Convicts were forcibly transported from England to work in the American colonies. In addition, thousands of African men, women, and children were kidnapped in Africa and forced onto slave ships. They were transported to America and forced to work for European masters. While voluntary emigrants had some choice of which territory they would move to, involuntary immigrants had no choice at all. Slaves were forced to immigrate to America from the 1500s until about 1840. For voluntary immigrants, two things influenced where they settled once they arrived in the United States. First, immigrants usually settled where there were jobs. Second, they often settled in the same places as immigrants who had come before them, especially those who were relatives or who had come from the same village or town in their homeland. This is called chain migration. Immigrants felt more comfortable living among people whose language they understood and whom they might have known in the "old country."

Immigrants often came to America with particular skills that they had learned in their native countries. These included occupations such as carpentry, butchering, jewelry making, metal machining, and farming. Immigrants settled in places where they could find jobs using these skills.

In addition to skills, immigrant groups brought their languages, religions, and customs with them to the new land. Each of these many cultures has made unique contributions to American life. Each group has added to the multicultural society that is America today.

Waves of Immigration

Many immigrant groups came to America in waves. In the early 1800s, economic conditions in Europe were growing harsh. Famine in Ireland led to a massive push of emigration of Irish men and women to the United States. A similar number of

German farmers and urban workers migrated to America. They were attracted by high wages, a growing number of jobs, and low land prices. Starting in 1880, huge numbers of people in southern and eastern Europe, including Italians, Russians, Poles, and Greeks, were facing rising populations and poor economies. To escape these conditions, they chose to immigrate to the United States. In the first 10 years of the 20th century, immigration from Europe was in the millions each year, with a peak of 8 million immigrants in 1910. In the 1930s, thousands of Jewish immigrants fled religious persecution in Nazi Germany and came to America.

Becoming a Legal Immigrant

There were few limits on the number of immigrants that could come to America until 1924. That year, Congress limited immigration to the United States to only 100,000 per year. In 1965, the number of immigrants allowed into the United States each year was raised from 100,000 to 290,000. In 1986, Congress further relaxed immigration rules, especially for immigrants from Cuba and Haiti. The new law allowed 1.5 million legal immigrants to enter the United States in 1990. Since then, more than half a million people have legally immigrated to the United States each year.

Not everyone who wants to immigrate to the United States is allowed to do so. The number of people from other countries who may immigrate to America is determined by a federal law called the Immigration and Naturalization Act (INA). This law was first passed in 1952. It has been amended (changed) many times since then.

Following the terrorist attacks on the World Trade Center in New York City and the Pentagon in Washington, D.C., in 2001, Congress made significant changes in the INA. One important change was to make the agency that administers laws concerning immigrants and other people entering the United States part of the Department of Homeland Security (DHS). The DHS is responsible for protecting the United States from attacks by terrorists. The new immigration agency is called the Citizenship and Immigration Service (CIS). It replaced the previous agency, which was called the Immigration and Naturalization Service (INS).

When noncitizens enter the United States, they must obtain official permission from the government to stay in the country. This permission is called a visa. Visas are issued by the CIS for a specific time period. In order to remain in the country permanently, an immigrant must obtain a permanent resident visa, also called a green card. This document allows a person to live, work, and study in the United States for an unlimited amount of time.

To qualify for a green card, an immigrant must have a sponsor. In most cases, a sponsor is a member of the immigrant's family who is a U.S. citizen or holds a green card. The government sets an annual limit of 226,000 on the number of family members who may be sponsored for permanent residence. In addition, no more than 25,650 immigrants may come from any one country.

In addition to family members, there are two other main avenues to obtaining a green card. A person may be sponsored by a U.S. employer or may enter the Green Card Lottery. An employer may sponsor a person who has unique work qualifications. The Green Card Lottery randomly selects 50,000 winners each year to receive green cards. Applicants for the lottery may be from any country from which immigration is allowed by U.S. law.

However, a green card does not grant an immigrant U.S. citizenship. Many immigrants have chosen to become citizens of the United States. Legal immigrants who have lived in the United States for at least five years and who meet other requirements may apply to become naturalized citizens. Once these immigrants qualify for citizenship, they become full-fledged citizens and have all the rights, privileges, and obligations of other U.S. citizens.

Even with these newer laws, there are always more people who want to immigrate to the United States than are allowed by law. As a result, some people choose to come to the United States illegally. Illegal immigrants do not have permission from the U.S. government to enter the country. Since 1980, the number of illegal immigrants entering the United States, especially from Central and South America, has increased greatly. These illegal immigrants are pushed by poverty in their homelands and pulled by the hope of a better life in the United States. Illegal immigration cannot be exactly measured, but it is believed that between 1 million and 3 million illegal immigrants enter the United States each year.

This series, Immigration to the United States, describes the history of the immigrant groups that have come to the United States. Some came because of the pull of America and the hope of a better life. Others were pushed out of their homelands. Still others were forced to immigrate as slaves. Whatever the reasons for their arrival, each group has a unique story and has made a unique contribution to the American way of life. 🎌

Right: Street vendors of all kinds, like this man (left) selling clams, were a common sight in immigrant neighborhoods of New York City in the early 20th century.

Introduction

Italian Immigration

Coming to America

Around the world, people who have never been to Italy know of its wonders. Italian art and music have touched millions with their beauty. The country's chefs and national dishes have delighted diners wherever Italians have settled.

One of the greatest empires of all time started in Italy's capital, Rome. The Roman Empire reached its peak in the second century A.D. Latin, the language of the empire, shaped many modern languages, including Italian. Countless English words also trace their roots to Latin. For centuries, Roman Catholic priests from Italy spread Christianity across Europe and other parts of the world.

The glories of the Roman Empire eventually faded. Italy came under foreign rule and broke apart into separate states. Italians, however, remained proud of their past, even as they began to seek work and new opportunities in foreign lands. Some of the first Europeans to reach the Far East, including China and Japan, were Italian. Some were merchants hoping to trade goods, while others were priests trying to spread their faith. Italians were also among the first Europeans to explore North and South America.

At first, only a few Italians settled in the colonies that became the United States. But by the early 20th century, Italy was sending more immigrants to the United States than any other country. Most Italian immigrants were peasants without much education. They were pushed from their homeland by extreme poverty, while the promise of jobs and a better life pulled them to America. Millions found what they were looking for in the United States and stayed.

These Italian immigrants often faced prejudice. Many Americans did not like the Italians' religion. Furthermore, Italian immigrants were often very poor and lived in cramped, crowded apartments, where diseases spread quickly. This made some Americans like them even less. Americans also began to associate Italian immigrants with crime, because a few of them were involved in illegal activities. In reality, however, Italians were no more likely to break the law than members of any other ethnic group. Italians as a whole worked hard, saved their money, and tried to become good Americans.

Like other immigrants, the Italians became Americans while trying to keep some of their old traditions. Italian Americans take pride in their culture and their ties to the country their families once called home. These millions of Italian Americans are also totally American, succeeding in business, politics, the arts, and every other part of U.S. society.

Opposite: *This portrait of Italian explorer Christopher Columbus (Cristoforo Colombo) was created in 1519, 27 years after his first voyage to the New World.*

Chapter One

Explorers and Early Immigrants

Italians in the New World

Italian Navigators

During the 15th century, several European nations started what has been called the Age of Exploration. Spain and Portugal took the lead by sending ships far from the well-known waters of the Mediterranean Sea. These vessels headed west into the Atlantic Ocean and south along the western coast of Africa. The rulers of Spain and Portugal hoped to boost their trade with India and other parts of Asia, the source of exotic spices and other valuable goods.

In 1492, a sea captain from Genoa, Italy, named Christopher Columbus was hired by Ferdinand and Isabella, the king and queen of Spain, to begin a historic voyage. Believing he could find a shorter route to China, Japan, and the Asian islands known as the Indies, Columbus sailed west instead of south along the coast of Africa.

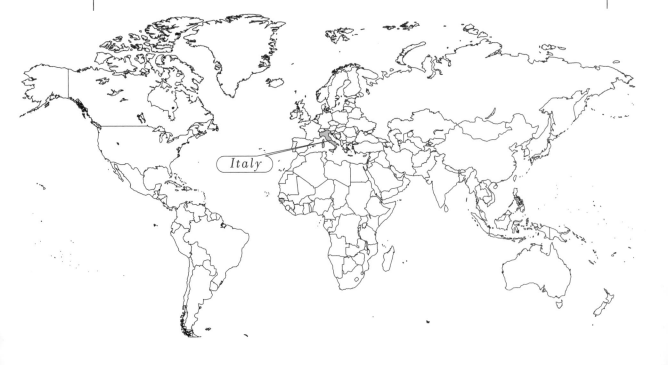

Italy

Polo's Role

Columbus, like many explorers at the time, learned about Asia from the experiences of an earlier Italian explorer, Marco Polo. From 1273 to 1293, Polo traveled across Asia while serving as an aide to Kublai Khan, the emperor of China. When he returned to Italy, Polo described his adventures to a writer who published a book about Polo's feats. Some sources say that Columbus carried a copy of that book with him on his first voyage across the Atlantic.

Columbus crossed the Atlantic Ocean and came ashore in what are now the islands of The Bahamas. He was convinced that he had reached Asia. Finally, after several more voyages, he realized that he had reached a territory no European of his era had ever seen before: the so-called New World. Columbus never landed on the mainland of North America. His explorations focused on Central America, South America, and the islands of the Caribbean Sea. Yet this brave Italian sea captain paved the way for the first permanent contact between Europe and North America.

> ## It's a Fact!
>
> In Italian, Christopher Columbus's name was Cristoforo Colombo.

New Explorations

In the years after Columbus, other Italians continued exploring the New World. In 1497, Giovanni Caboto sailed from England, working for King Henry VII. Caboto, better known by his English name, John Cabot, claimed what is now Newfoundland, Canada, for the English king.

The name "America" for the New World came from the first name of Italian navigator Amerigo Vespucci (1454–1519), pictured above.

Two years later, Italian explorer Amerigo Vespucci made the first of two voyages to North and South America, sailing for Spain. His trips took him past what is now the east coast of the United States. Vespucci wrote about his trips, and a German mapmaker suggested that the large landmass of the New World be named for Vespucci. His first name, Amerigo, led to the name "America."

A fourth Italian explorer, Giovanni da Verrazano, reached North America in 1524. Like Columbus, he thought he could find a shortcut to Asia by traveling west from Europe. Sailing for France, Verrazano was the first European to explore what is now New York Harbor. In a letter to the French king, Francis I, Verrazano called the bay where he dropped anchor a "most beautiful lake."

Italians in Colonial America

Sailors were not the only Italians to leave their homeland and work for foreigners. Educated people from the northern part of Italy, such as doctors and scientists, often found work in the kingdoms of Europe. So did artists, entertainers, and artisans, who were people who created jewelry, pottery, and other useful items of everyday life. Italians from the south, ruled by a French and Spanish royal family called the Bourbons, were not allowed to travel freely and could not emigrate.

By the mid-16th century, the leading Italian cities began to lose their economic and political power and their independence. Spain held the greatest influence over the country. Later, Austria played a major role in the northern regions. As the northern Italian cities declined, more skilled Italians began to seek jobs in other parts of Europe. Workers with fewer skills, on the other hand, sometimes joined foreign navies and armies. In this way, more Italians reached the New World. Italians fought for Spain as that country set up colonies in Florida. They also traveled with the Spanish as missionaries—Roman Catholic priests sent to teach Christianity to the American Indians.

In 1607, England established a colony in North America, joining its rivals France and Spain, which had already started colonies there. English settlers landed in Virginia and founded the town of Jamestown. About 15 years later, officials in the colony wanted help making glass, so they invited some Italian glassmakers from Venice to settle in Jamestown. These skilled craftsmen were among the first Italians to be pulled to America seeking a better life.

Italian Priest and Explorer

Perhaps the first Italian missionary in North America was Marco da Nizza (in Spanish, Marcos de Niza), a priest from Nice, which was once part of the northern Italian kingdom of Savoy. Working for the Spanish government, da Nizza went to Mexico, at that time a Spanish colony, during the 1530s. In March 1539, he traveled north to the region that is now the southern part of Arizona and New Mexico. Returning to Mexico, the priest told Spanish officials about a Native American city that was supposedly filled with riches. That report led to the first major Spanish expedition from Mexico into what is now the United States.

Some Italians were drawn to colonial America for religious reasons. Most Italians in the 17th century belonged to the Roman Catholic Church. Italy also had a tiny number of Protestants, but they could not freely practice their faith in their

Catholic homeland. One group of Italian Protestants, the Waldensians, lost their legal rights and at times faced execution for their beliefs. In 1657, a group of Waldensians came to New York City (then called New Amsterdam), so they could worship as they chose.

Explorers in America

During the last half of the 17th century, other important Italians came to America. One, Enrico di Tonti, was a sailor and explorer who was working for the French government when he reached America in 1678. Tonti sailed with the better-known French explorer Robert Cavelier de La Salle. Together, the two men and their crew sailed down the Mississippi River and claimed Louisiana for France.

It's a Fact!

Enrico di Tonti's brother Alphonse came to America in 1701 and helped found the city of Detroit, Michigan.

Along the Mississippi River, Tonti helped build Fort St. Louis, in what is now Illinois. From there, he carried on a booming fur trade with the region's Native Americans. The tribes respected Tonti, who was known as "the man with the iron hand" after he lost his right hand in battle and replaced it with a metal one. Tonti started a second trading fort farther south along the Mississippi, and he dealt with Native Americans from as far away as Hudson's Bay in Canada and the American Southwest. Father St. Cosme, a French missionary to the region, wrote in a letter that Tonti "best knows the country . . . he is loved and feared everywhere."

Francesco Bressani, an Italian missionary, also came to North America. Bressani, a priest, did most of his work in Canada, but he also traveled through upstate New York. According to Italian-American historian Giovanni Schiavo, Bressani was the first

European to describe Niagara Falls. In addition, he created some of the first maps and drawings of Indian life in North America. In 1644, Bressani was captured by Native Americans but won his freedom in Albany, New York, with the help of Dutch settlers. Bressani wrote a detailed account of his years living with the Huron and neighboring Native American tribes in the region.

Throughout the colonial period, several thousand Italians reached the thirteen British colonies that later became the United States. Like the earlier Italians who left their homeland and settled in Europe, these immigrants usually had specific skills. They came to the American colonies hoping to build successful careers. During the 1730s, for example, a small group of Italian silk workers came to Georgia. The colony's founder, James Oglethorpe, hoped to create a silk industry and needed the expertise of these immigrants. Italians also excelled as musicians, and some came to America to teach and perform.

The American Revolution

By the early 1770s, some Americans in the colonies were protesting the British government that ruled them. Those protests led to the American Revolution. Italian immigrants played important roles in fighting that war.

Philip Mazzei, for instance, was a surgeon and a farmer in Italy who applied scientific methods to raising crops. He was also a merchant, and in 1756 he moved to London, where he met several Americans. One of them was Benjamin Franklin. A printer, politician, and scientist, Franklin

It's a Fact!

When he came to America, Philip Mazzei brought grapes from Italy, hoping to create a wine industry. He also brought other Italian products to Virginia, including olives and citrus fruit.

often represented the colonies in Great Britain. Franklin and other Americans convinced Mazzei to go to Virginia and set up an experimental farm to grow Italian crops. Mazzei reached the colony in 1773, when more and more Americans were challenging British laws that limited their freedom. Mazzei quickly became friends with some of the leading political figures in Virginia, including Thomas Jefferson.

Mazzei strongly believed in democracy and equal rights. He began spending less time on his farm and more on politics, writing and speaking about the colonies' struggles with Great Britain. In one of his articles, Mazzei wrote, "All men are by nature equally free and independent." Later, Thomas Jefferson used a similar phrase when he wrote the Declaration of Independence: "All men are created equal." Mazzei's ideas on politics and society clearly influenced the leaders of the Revolution. After the Revolutionary War began, Mazzei traveled to Europe for the new United States government. He was seeking money and supplies from friendly governments there. After the war, he became the first European to write a history of the founding of the United States.

What's in a Name?

Historians trying to track down early Italian immigrants in America face a problem. Some of the immigrants did not come directly to North America from Italy and changed their names in Europe or once they reached America. During the colonial era, some Italian immigrants became naturalized, or legal, citizens of England. A list of some of these people includes several names that are not Italian, such as Foxe, John, Grey, and Benson. In some cases, Italian names were made to sound English. Taliaferro, for example, might be written as Talifer or Tolliver. Centuries later, some Italian-American immigrants also changed their names to sound more like English names.

Another important Italian during the American Revolution was Francesco Vigo. He had come to America as a soldier working for Spain and then entered the fur trade, working along the banks of the Mississippi River. In 1778, Vigo began working with George Rogers Clark, a U.S. general pre-paring to attack British forces in the Midwest. While on a trade mission for Clark, Vigo was captured by the British. He spent several weeks at Vincennes, in what is now Indiana, the main British fort in the region. After the British released him, Vigo gave Clark details on the fort and the British defenses there. Clark used that information to launch a surprise attack that led to a major U.S. victory. Vigo had performed an important role for Clark, acting as the general's spy. After the Revolution, Vigo settled in Vincennes and is believed to be the first Italian to become a U.S. citizen.

Mazzei and Vigo were the most famous Italians to help Americans win the Revolutionary War, but they were not alone. Other Italians fought as common soldiers and a group of Italian soldiers also fought for France, which sent troops to aid the Americans.

William Paca was one of two men of Italian heritage who signed the Declaration of Independence in 1776. He is pictured here in 1780.

It's a Fact!

Lorenzo Da Ponte worked with the 18th-century Austrian composer Wolfgang Amadeus Mozart to write some of the world's most famous operas. Da Ponte wrote the words set to Mozart's music. In the early 1800s, Da Ponte came to New York and promoted professional opera in the United States.

Independent Italians

At the time of the American Revolution, most colonial leaders, and most Americans in general, came from English, Irish, or Scottish backgrounds. For that reason, many Americans believed that everyone who signed the Declaration of Independence also shared those ethnic ties. During the 20th century, however, historians learned that two of the signers had Italian roots. One was William Paca of Maryland. In Italy, Paca's family's name may have been either Pacci or Pecci. During the Revolution, Paca used some of his own money to supply American troops. Paca was also the first Italian-American governor, holding that position in Maryland from 1782 to 1785. Caesar Rodney also traced his Italian roots through his father, though his last name sounded English. Rodney, from Delaware, held several political offices and also served as a general during the American Revolution. Rodney is best known for a midnight ride he made to cast Delaware's deciding vote in support of the Declaration of Independence.

Italians in the New Republic

With its victory over Great Britain in 1783, the United States won its independence. In the next few decades, the number of Italian immigrants to the new country remained small compared to the number who came from England, Ireland, and Germany. In 1820, for example, the U.S. government recorded the arrival of just 30 people from Italy. Fewer than 500 came between 1821 and 1830.

As in the past, the Italians who did come to the United States during this time tended to have specialized skills. Italy has a long tradition as the home of talented painters, sculptors, and musicians, and such Italian artists often found work in the United States. Several business owners also came, along with merchants and artisans. Most of these immigrants settled in the Northeast or in and around New Orleans, Louisiana. By 1850 more Italian immigrants lived in Louisiana than in any other state.

Many immigrants, including Italians, poured into California after gold was discovered there in 1848. They worked at digging and processing gold and hoped to strike it rich.

A Forgotten Inventor

When Antonio Meucci died in 1889, a New York newspaper praised him for his skills as an inventor. Some people claim Meucci never received credit for his greatest invention: the telephone. For decades, he tried to find a way to use electricity to transmit the human voice over a wire. In 1860, Meucci gave a public demonstration of his "speaking telegraph." Meucci hoped to receive a patent for his invention, but he lost his papers and models before he could complete the process. Instead of Meucci winning praise as the inventor of the telephone, Alexander Graham Bell received a patent for the device in 1876.

In 1848, events in Europe led to an increase in Italian immigration to the United States. Italy was divided into several small states, while Austria controlled large parts of the north. The Italians, like many other Europeans at the time, were ruled by kings or princes. Citizens eager for democratic governments rebelled against their leaders.

Across Europe, however, the royal rulers crushed the rebellions. Some Italians fled to Great Britain and the United States. Many of these immigrants hoped to return one day to a free and united Italy. Others, however, made the United States their permanent home. Between 1851 and 1860, more than 9,000 Italians entered the country. This was more than had arrived during the previous three decades combined.

In 1848, gold was discovered in California, and the gold rush that followed attracted immigrants from all over the world. Only a few made their fortunes mining gold, but thousands stayed to pursue other careers. Many of the first Italians in California farmed or fished for a living, while others went into business. The farmers grew crops not commonly found in the United States, such as artichokes and eggplants, and herbs such as fennel and rosemary.

The Civil War

B y 1860, the U.S. Census (an official count of the population done by the U.S. government) reported that about 10,000 Italians lived in the United States. (The total U.S. population that year was 28 million.) Most of these immigrants had come from northern Italy. By this time, the Italian-American communities in San Francisco and New York City had their own newspapers printed in Italian, and several Italians were successful in business and local politics.

In 1861, the United States faced the most serious crisis since its founding. Eleven Southern states formed a new country, the Confederate States of America. President Abraham Lincoln declared that the states did not have the right to leave the Union—the United States. He prepared Union troops for a war against the South, and soon after, the Civil War (1861–1865) began.

During the Civil War, Italian Americans fought on both sides, though most lived in the North and sided with the Union. In New York City, a group of Italian-American volunteers formed a military unit that fought throughout the war. Several Italians served as officers on both sides.

The war ended in 1865 with the defeat of the Confederacy and reunification of the country. In the decade of the Civil War, the number of Italians arriving in the United States reached its highest level until that time. On average, more than 1,000 new immigrants came each year. The 1870s saw that number increase more than five times. These new arrivals began to mark a shift in the Italian immigrant population. Changes within Italy led to changes in who left the country for the United States, and why. ✤

Opposite: *An Italian immigrant family arrives at Ellis Island in New York Harbor in 1905.*

Chapter Two

The First
Great Wave

1880–1900

Conditions in Italy

Through the 1850s and 1860s, Italians in northern and central Italy continued the fight to end foreign control of their homeland. By 1870, they achieved their goal. For the first time in centuries, Italy was united under an Italian government.

Independence and unity meant changes for many Italian citizens, especially the peasant farmers of the south. This region includes all the territory south of Naples, as well as the islands of Sicily and Sardinia. The Italians called this southern region the Mezzogiorno. With the new government, Italians in the Mezzogiorno were finally free to travel. That legal freedom, along with several other key factors, led to mass emigration over the next few decades.

It's a Fact!

The word *mezzogiorno* is Italian for "midday." As the name of the southern region of Italy, the word refers to the hot midday sun that beats down there.

Life in the Mezzogiorno

For centuries, most southern Italians had worked as tenant farmers, meaning that they raised crops on land owned by distant landlords. Most of the farmers were uneducated and had almost no chance to find better work. They remained peasants their entire lives. Farming in the region was never easy, as the land was mountainous and rain was scarce during the summer and fall.

After 1870, the peasants of the Mezzogiorno had new demands in their already difficult lives. The government introduced new taxes and required young men to serve in the military. The price for Italian wheat fell, as other countries increased their production of this important grain. Falling prices meant less money for Italian farmers, who could barely keep their families fed. A poor family might have meat only a few times a year, on holidays. Most meals featured beans and some type of grain. During the 1880s, a disease called cholera swept through Italy, killing more than 50,000 people. Natural disasters such as earthquakes and landslides also struck, destroying towns. As life grew harsher, many Italians decided they had to leave their homeland.

In general, the Italian government at the time was dominated by northerners. Their region of Italy was wealthier and more modern than the south. Most northerners disliked the poor, uneducated peasants of the Mezzogiorno and did not support government policies that would help the region grow. They also did not welcome southern farmers and their families in northern cities.

When the southern Italians looked for new economic opportunities, they focused on foreign lands. While some went to other European nations for work, a growing number turned their attention across the Atlantic Ocean, to America. Most were not eager to go. As one Italian government official put it, the immigrants were "leaving in tears, cursing the government and the *signori* [landowners]." Political and economic difficulties were pushing the peasants out of their homeland.

The United States, meanwhile, offered jobs that unskilled, uneducated Italian peasants could do. The United States was growing rapidly during the 19th century, and there was often a shortage of workers. Immigrants from all nations filled that demand. Peasant farmers used to hard work in the Mezzogiorno, for example, took jobs building railroads and constructing buildings, while others took factory jobs that required little or no skill.

For the poorest Italians, horse-drawn carts were the main source of transportation in the late 1800s. This family from Sicily was photographed around 1900.

Coming to America

C hanges in transportation made the trip out of Italy easier than it had been in the past. Railway lines reached farther into the Italian countryside, so peasants could more easily reach the major port cities, such as Naples, Genoa, and Palermo. The poorest people, however, still relied on horse- or donkey-drawn carts to move them and their belongings to the docks.

At the ports, steamships replaced the old sailing ships that once carried immigrants across the Atlantic. Although the journey west was now quicker, it was still difficult for most

Italian immigrants. They traveled in steerage, the cheapest and worst class of service for passengers. The immigrants slept below the main decks in cramped, dark cabins. Whenever they could, the passengers came out on deck for fresh air, taking turns in the small space they were allowed. Few immigrants died on the transatlantic journey, but many spent their days seasick.

Italians arrived in the United States at a number of port cities, including Boston, Massachusetts; Baltimore, Maryland; New Orleans, Louisiana; and San Francisco, California. Most, however, came through New York City. After 1892, their first stop in New York City was Ellis Island. Located in New York Harbor, Ellis Island was the U.S. government's main center for processing immigrants. At the island, Italian immigrants were questioned about their job and housing prospects and received medical exams. After 1917, they had to prove they could read. Immigrants who did not have any money or who failed any of the tests were deported, or sent back to Italy.

For immigrants of all nationalities, going through Ellis Island could be a difficult experience. Some had to wait weeks before they were allowed to leave the island, while government officials checked their background. Immigrants who were sick had to stay at Ellis Island until their health improved. During the questioning process, families were sometimes separated, or one member might be denied admission. According to Ben Morreale and Jerre Mangione, in their history of Italian immigration, *La Storia,* the Italians called Ellis Island *l'isola dell lagrime,* which means "the island of tears."

The immigrants who received permission to enter the United States took a ferry from Ellis Island to Manhattan, a part of

It's a Fact!

Ellis Island was open for 62 years. During that time, slightly more than 2.5 million Italians entered the United States there, the highest number of any ethnic group.

New York City. Usually family members or friends who had already emigrated greeted them as they arrived. With their help, the new immigrants got jobs, found places to live, and learned their first words of English. Life was harder, however, for the immigrants who did not know anyone in America. Most did not speak English and they usually arrived with little money. They had come from tiny farming villages, but now they faced a large, noisy, crowded city. These lonely immigrants often accepted help from any stranger who spoke Italian and offered aid. In some cases, the strangers actually wanted to rob or cheat them, adding to the immigrants' problems.

Birds of Passage

During the 1880s and 1890s, most of the Italian immigrants in America were men between the ages of 15 and 45. Many of them were so-called birds of passage. They worked part of the year in the United States, then either returned to Italy or traveled to another warm climate during the winter. The next year, the men would come back to the United States. Wherever they worked, the birds of passage sent money home to their families in Italy.

Sometimes a man returned to his homeland with a special purpose. Called a padrone (boss), he recruited other Italians to emigrate to the United States. The padrone promised the workers jobs and help with adjusting to life in a foreign land. The Italian boss also sometimes paid for the immigrants' voyage across the Atlantic. In return, the

It's a Fact

From 1881 to 1890, more than 300,000 Italians entered the United States. The number more than doubled during the next decade. Most of these immigrants were from the Mezzogiorno.

padrone took a percentage of the money the workers earned. Many padrones took advantage of the workers they recruited. They charged high interest on loans they made and required the workers to pay fees for the padrones' help in finding housing and rides to work.

The padrones' treatment of many newcomers led Congress to pass a law in 1885 that tried to end the padrone system. The bosses, however, found ways around the law and continued to take advantage of immigrants. Some padrones, however, did provide real help to immigrants who did not understand American society.

Settling In

Not all Italian immigrants were birds of passage. Some sent money back to Italy so their families could afford to join them in America. Others went back to Italy to find brides, then returned to the United States to start families. Whenever the immigrants returned to Italy, they described their life in *Lamerica,* as the Italians called it. They explained that life could be hard, with low-paying jobs and harsh living conditions. Many, however, went back to Italy with more money than they had ever earned in the Mezzogiorno. The idea of newfound wealth kept feeding the stream of immigrants to the United States.

Many of the newcomers headed for the cities where earlier immigrants from their villages had settled. This pattern was known as chain migration. Within a particular city, the Italians tended to live in certain neighborhoods. In New York City, for example, the area around Mulberry Street, on the Lower East Side, developed into a "Little Italy." Other cities had their own versions of these Italian neighborhoods. Within these neighborhoods, people from the same village settled near each other.

*Italians and other immigrants often lived, and sometimes worked,
in crowded tenement buildings like this one on Elizabeth Street on
New York City's Lower East Side.*

In Italy, Italian social and political life focused on the village. Italians sometimes talked of *campanilismo*. A campanile is a church bell tower. *Campanilismo* referred to the idea that only the people who could hear the sound of the local church bell could be trusted. Anyone beyond that range was a stranger who posed a potential threat to the local community. *Campanilismo* came with the immigrants to the United States, shaping where the new arrivals lived. Enrico Sartorio, an Italian-American scholar, noted early in the 20th century, "In the heart of the nearest city, one can find in the Italian colony a Sicilian, a Calabrian, a Neapolitan, an Abruzzian village, all within a few blocks, and each with its peculiar traditions, manner of living, and dialect."

The living conditions in these Italian neighborhoods could be harsh. Just as earlier immigrants had done, the Italians crowded into apartment buildings called tenements. Most tenements were in slums, areas of the city that lacked public sanitation and where crime tended to be high. The apartments were arranged with one room behind another, like cars on a train, and most rooms lacked windows. A whole family or up to ten single men might share one room, and a family might take in boarders to help pay expenses. The buildings themselves were packed close together, with little light or fresh air. Such living conditions led to frequent illness, such as the lung disease tuberculosis. In summer, many people slept on the roof of their building to escape the heat. Parents often let their children play in the street until late at night, when the temperature inside the apartment might have cooled down. In winter, many Italians shivered in unheated apartments.

To escape the harsh life in the tenements, Italians turned to activities outside the home. Italian-language theaters sprang up in the Little Italy sections of cities across the country. Amateur actors staged plays to entertain their friends and neighbors. Later, some professional actors translated English-language plays into Italian. The Italian theaters of New York and other cities inspired some Italian-American actors who went on to become stars in American theater and in films. Puppet theaters were also popular in Italian neighborhoods, as puppetry had a long tradition in Italy. The story of the puppet boy named Pinocchio who came to life was written by an Italian named Carlo Lorenzini (Collodi) in 1881.

The conditions in the tenements led many Italians to move into better neighborhoods as soon as they could. The lure of better jobs also led some to move out of New York, where most new arrivals settled, to other parts of the United States. Other popular destinations for the immigrants of the 1880s and 1890s were Boston, Chicago, mill towns in New England, and coal towns of the Midwest.

Italian immigrants went wherever there was work to be done.
These workers in upstate New York were helping to build
a railroad around 1900.

Finding Work

Most of the new arrivals from the Mezzogiorno had worked as farmers. In the United States, however, most of the farmers gave up hope of raising crops as they had in Italy. They lacked the money to buy land, and the only jobs they could get were in the cities and towns, not on farms.

Italians by the thousands helped build railroads and other important parts of America's transportation system. They worked on the Brooklyn Bridge and dug the tunnels for New York's subways. Men and women worked for small clothing companies or factories that made cheap jewelry and other inexpensive items. At night, they took home materials so they and their families could continue to assemble finished goods. In this system, called piecework, the workers were paid for each item they finished instead of by the hour. One unnamed immigrant, quoted by Jerre Mangione and Ben Morreale in *La Storia*, remembered working in his kitchen with his parents, making jewelry: "We worked until after midnight but never after one. At least I wouldn't for I had to go to school in the morning."

Other Italian immigrants opened small stores (particularly grocery stores) or barbershops. In fact, a large percentage of barbers in America at that time were Italian. Many Italian immigrants became tailors. A number of northern Italians went to New England during the 1880s to work as granite stonecutters. A pattern of chain migration brought many of these workers to the town of Barre, Vermont. Italians were known for their skill at carving the stones and using them in landscaping.

Mr. Peanut's Italian Roots

One Italian immigrant who found work on the streets of America was Amedeo Obici. In 1887, the 11-year-old left Venice, Italy, and settled in Pennsylvania. One of his first jobs was selling fruit from a street stand. In the city of Wilkes-Barre, Obici began selling bags of roasted peanuts on the street for a nickel. In 1906, he went into business with another Italian immigrant, Mario Peruzzi, and two years later they started the Planters Nut and Chocolate Company. Obici's major breakthrough was selling shelled and roasted peanuts in small bags. He also introduced one of the best-known images in U.S. advertising: Mr. Peanut. The human-like peanut with a face, arms, and legs first appeared in 1916 to promote Planters products. Planters nuts and Mr. Peanut can still be seen on store shelves today.

Some Italians were able to find work in farming, and some found jobs on the water. A large farming community developed in California during the 1870s. In addition to growing fruits and vegetables, Italian immigrants helped turn the state into one of the world's leading wine-producing regions. In New Orleans, Italian merchants dominated the selling and transporting of fruits and vegetables. And Italian fishers created their own communities in several cities, including San Francisco, California and Galveston, Texas.

Immigrants entering the United States were required to present a passport such as this one, issued to an Italian immigrant in 1890. Passports identified the immigrants and their country of origin.

Reaction to the Italians

The growing numbers of Italian immigrants in the 1880s and 1890s were part of a changing pattern of immigration in the United States. The Italians were soon lumped with people from southern and eastern Europe as "new immigrants." Americans saw a distinction between these immigrants and the "old" arrivals, who had come mainly from Great Britain, Ireland, Germany, and Scandinavia (Norway, Sweden, and Denmark). The old immigrants were primarily Protestant and fair-skinned. The new immigrants tended to be either Jewish or Catholic, and they often had darker skin.

These religious and physical differences, as well as other factors, led some native-born Americans to discriminate against the new immigrants. These Americans were often called nativists.

Some Americans hated the Italians because they acted as strikebreakers. In the last three decades of the 19th century, American workers began to strike, or refuse to work unless they received higher pay and better working conditions. To keep factories and mines running, company owners often brought in new workers called strikebreakers. With replacement workers to keep the factories and mines going, business owners did not have to give their striking workers the better pay and conditions they were demanding. Italians needed the work and would accept lower pay than the native-born Americans. By working as strikebreakers, the immigrants fed their families, but earned the hatred of the striking workers they replaced.

The padrone system was another reason that some native-born Americans disliked Italian immigrants. For some Americans, the padrones who acted illegally in their business dealings created the impression that Italians were prone to commit crime. In the popular view, Italians were more violent than members of other ethnic groups. They were said to settle their arguments with knives, and one expert in crime wrote in 1890, "[the Italian] is quite as familiar with the sight of human blood as with the sight of the food he eats." The popular image, however, hid the reality: In general, Italian immigrants were not more likely to commit crimes than any other foreign-born residents of the United States.

A True Saint

Tales of life in the crowded tenements and dangerous neighborhoods of New York traveled back to Italy. After hearing about the harsh conditions, an Italian nun named Frances Xavier Cabrini came to the United States in 1889 to help Italian immigrants.

Mother Cabrini, as she was known, started schools, orphanages, hospitals, and convents (homes for Roman Catholic nuns). She eventually became a U.S. citizen and, in 1946, became the first U.S. citizen to be named a saint in the Catholic Church.

Despite the extreme prejudice they faced, most Italians who stayed in the United States wanted to be good citizens. Some took an interest in politics and government. In 1886, Francis Spinola became the first Italian American elected to the U.S. Congress. By the start of the 20th century, Italian Americans had served as mayors, and one, Andrew Longino, was elected governor of Mississippi. These successful politicians showed that not all Americans distrusted Italians and that, as a group, Italians had something positive to offer their new country.

Opposite: *New immigrants celebrate on the deck of their ship as the Statue of Liberty comes into view in 1915.*

Chapter Three

The Peak Years

1900–1920

Immigration Increases

As the 20th century began, Italians continued to stream into the United States, averaging just over 200,000 per year between 1901 and 1910. The number fell slightly during the next decade, primarily because of World War I. The war, which lasted from 1914 to 1918, disrupted travel between Europe and the United States. Still, 1.1 million Italians reached the United States between 1911 and 1920.

The reasons for the immigration had not changed. Bad economic conditions in Italy, especially in the Mezzogiorno, pushed many Italians to seek new opportunities. A disease called malaria was also a problem, killing up to 20,000 people every year. Furthermore, the United States still pulled immigrants with the promise of jobs and a chance to make more money than most of them could earn in their homeland. The trip across the Atlantic Ocean was also more affordable for many than it had been before, thanks to the money the first Italian immigrants sent home. During 1901, the typical Italian-American immigrant sent $250 back to relatives in Italy. That money, equivalent to about $5,700 today, could pay for an ocean voyage or make life easier for family members who decided to stay in Italy.

Although more immigrants could now afford their passage to America, conditions for the new arrivals had not changed much. Most took whatever jobs they could find, especially in construction. In 1921, Constantine Panunzio wrote about his experiences when he had first arrived in Boston almost two

It's a Fact!

From 1880 to 1920, more immigrants to the United States came from Italy than from any other country. During that time, the total number of Italians entering the country was slightly more than 4 million.

decades before. "We began to make inquiries about jobs," he wrote, "and were promptly informed that there was plenty of work at 'pick and shovel.'" Panunzio, like most new arrivals, did not speak any English, but he assumed "pick and shovel" was some kind of office job. He was disappointed to learn that his new job involved digging a ditch.

Most of the new arrivals continued to live in cities in the Northeast. The 1920 census reported that almost 85 percent of all Italian Americans lived in cities. New York City remained the center of the Italian-American population. In 1917, the city had about 700,000 Italian Americans. Roughly half were first generation, meaning that they were born in Italy, while the rest were second generation, or born in the United States.

Some Italians did go to rural areas, primarily to farm. The Italian wine-making community in California continued to grow, and Italian farmers prospered in Texas and Louisiana. Farming communities also developed in the Northeast. In 1909, Vineland, New Jersey, had the largest community of Italian-American farmers in the country. The settlement had been founded during the 1870s, when the American landowner there specifically recruited Italians to work the land. The farmers raised grapes, strawberries, beans, and peppers.

Family Life

Although most Italian immigrants of this period were still single men, more and more Italian families were arriving together. In Italy, the family played a large role in most Italians' lives, and that role was even more important in the United States. Living in a foreign country and often facing discrimination, most Italian Americans believed that the only people they could trust were their relatives.

The center of this circle of relatives was the mother, father, and their children. Also important was the extended family of grandparents, aunts, uncles, and cousins. Within the family, the father was considered the head. The other members of the family, especially the children, were supposed to accept his decisions. Even adult children were expected to follow their father's advice and obey him. An adult son who still lived at home usually gave his parents his paycheck, and they would give him a weekly allowance. Adult daughters had limited freedom outside of the home, and the family played a role in choosing whom they would marry.

Although the father was the "king" of the household, the mother also played an important role. She usually controlled the family's finances, and she might challenge her husband's decisions if she disagreed, though only in private. In public, she also accepted his rule.

The Malatestas, an Italian immigrant family, make artificial flower bouquets around the table in their tenement apartment in 1908. They were paid according to how many bouquets they produced.

Family Finances

Italian Americans of the early 20th century were well known for their willingness to work hard and save money. In 1904, Italian-American lawyer Gino Speranza wrote that, in New York City, Italians owned 10,000 stores and had more than $15 million saved in local banks. About 15 years later, an Italian-American economics professor, John Horace Mariano, noted that "industry and thrift . . . are innate traits of the Italian family." He said that Italian Americans in New York City owned property worth at least $100 million.

In Italy, children were expected to begin helping on the farm or in a family business when they were 10 or 11 years old. In the United States, many young Italian children also worked to help their families. Boys might sell papers or shine shoes, while girls helped with piecework or took jobs in factories. The girls, however, tended to be older if and when they took jobs outside the home, given the traditional Italian desire to protect girls from strangers.

Many Italian-American parents had mixed feelings about sending their children to school. They worried that their children would become too Americanized and lose their traditional culture and loyalty to the family. On the other hand, many Italian parents did not speak English, and they relied on their children to learn the language and help them survive in their new homeland.

An important part of family life was gathering for meals. Meals on Sundays and holidays included the extended family, with grandparents, aunts, uncles, and cousins. A typical Italian meal featured macaroni, which included pasta of all shapes and sizes. Pasta existed in the United States before the huge Italian immigration of the late 19th century, but the immigrants made it part of American cooking. As Italians opened restaurants, they introduced Americans to other common Italian foods. These included cheeses such as parmesan, mozzarella, and ricotta, and cold cuts such as salami and a special ham called prosciutto. Northern Italians often ate a simple corn dish called polenta. Today, it often appears in fancy American restaurants. Many Americans enjoy typical Italian "peasant food" because it is healthy and simple to make.

Speaking Italian

Spaghetti is just one of the many forms of pasta that now appear on store shelves. Italians, however, make their pasta in all shapes and sizes. A pasta's name often refers to its shape, such as *mostaccioli,* or "small moustaches." Other kinds of pasta sold today in the United States also have very descriptive names.

- **farfalle:** "butterfly"
- **vermicelli:** "little worms"
- **fettuccine:** "little ribbons"
- **linguine:** "small tongues"
- **orecchiette:** "little ears"

Religious Life

Within the family, Italians passed on the folklore and customs of their native land. Most also stayed in the Roman Catholic Church, historically the most important faith in Italy. The immigrants' religious life was centered on weekly mass, or church service, and various holidays that featured large celebrations. Christmas and Easter were two of those important days, but the Italians also celebrated the birthdays of saints. In Italy, people from different towns and regions honored different saints with *feste,* or public celebrations. A *festa* was a religious event, but it was also a social occasion, featuring food, music, and games. In the United States, the Italians continued this tradition. One of the most important *feste* honored Saint Joseph, the father of Jesus Christ. In 1922, an observer described the "decoration, street illumination, and fireworks for the processions" that marked a typical *festa.*

Although most Italians considered themselves religious, they were often not as strict about following church rules as other Catholic Americans. Italians also did not see any conflict between their religious beliefs and superstitions. Superstitions are beliefs or fears based on magic or other forces that cannot be readily explained. Many religions teach people not to believe in superstitions. However, many Italian immigrants brought superstitions with them from the old country.

Among the first Italian arrivals to the United States, many from the Mezzogiorno believed in the *malocchio,* or "evil eye." Certain people were thought to have the power to create bad luck or illness by looking at someone in an evil way. Potential victims could avoid the evil eye by making certain hand gestures or hanging up horns from certain animals, such as a bull. Some people wore small horns around their neck to protect themselves from the evil eye.

> # It's a Fact!
>
> On Christmas Eve, many Italian-American families ate meatless meals. Some ate fish, including eels and smelts, while others might have only vegetables. Not eating meat was seen as a sacrifice in honor of Christ's birth.

The Italians' Banker

One of the most successful Italian-American business owners of the early 20th century was Amadeo Giannini. He was born in California in 1870 and entered banking as a young man. In 1904, he opened his own bank, Banca d'Italia, in San Francisco. His first customers were from that city's large Italian community. In 1906, San Francisco suffered a devastating earthquake, followed by a huge fire. Giannini was able to rescue the bank's money and business records before the building burned. He helped his customers rebuild their lives after the fire destroyed much of San Francisco. Giannini's bank eventually expanded across California and into other states. His Banca d'Italia became Bank of America, and it was a multibillion-dollar enterprise when Giannini died in 1949. Today, Bank of America is one of the top financial companies in the United States.

Outside the Home

Although Italian Americans focused on their families, many had ties with groups and organizations outside of their homes and neighborhoods. As early as the 1820s, Italian immigrants, like members of other ethnic groups, formed mutual aid societies. These societies helped immigrants who faced economic or social problems when they settled in the United States. Members paid dues; then the society helped them if they were sick or paid for a funeral when a member died. By 1915, Italian Americans had formed more than 2,000 mutual aid societies across the United States.

Many of the first Italian mutual aid societies were organized locally, but during the early 1900s, Italian Americans formed several societies with a larger focus. The first was the Order Sons of Italy in America (OSIA), founded in 1905. OSIA combined smaller existing mutual aid societies into a larger organization. Its goals, the organization's constitution said, included "keep[ing] alive the spiritual attachment to the traditions of the land of our ancestors" while encouraging immigrants to take part in politics and other public activities.

Italians also formed social and athletic clubs, where members met to talk and play games. Many social gatherings included boccie. This form of outdoor bowling was developed in Italy and remains a popular game with Italian Americans. Social clubs also held dances and picnics for members and their families. Italian-American members of certain professions, such as medicine or teaching, also formed their own clubs.

Moving Beyond the Ethnic Community

Through the first decades of the 1900s, many Italian Americans took part in what some historians call acculturation. This process involves the immigrants' adopting some parts of the culture of their new homeland. At the same time, the Italians and other immigrants dealt with a related process, called assimilation. Through assimilation, Italians lost some sense of their being a separate ethnic group and became more American. American culture itself also slowly changed as it accepted some of the traits of the Italians and other ethnic groups in the country. Individual immigrants became assimilated as they joined the workforce, went to school, and joined organizations that were not based on nationality.

For Italians, political parties and labor unions, which supported workers and their fight for better pay and working conditions, were part of their acculturation and assimilation. These organizations, unlike mutual aid societies, forced Italians to meet and deal with native-born Americans and other immigrants. The Italians, who tended to be suspicious of strangers, were slow to take active roles in politics and labor. They also distrusted powerful people, remembering how political leaders and bosses had abused them in Italy. And like other new immigrants, many Italians did not readily join groups outside of their nationality because they did not speak English well. But gradually Italian Americans joined political organizations and labor unions, sometimes moving into leadership positions.

Italians came to see the value of unions and of working together to improve conditions. They were less likely to be strikebreakers, as some new arrivals had been during the 1870s and 1880s.

Armed guards keep strikers away from the textile mill during the 1912 strike at Lawrence, Massachusetts. This strike was organized with the help of two Italian Americans.

Immigration's Effect on Italy

With so many of its citizens leaving for the United States, Italy saw both good and bad effects. In some small villages, not enough men remained behind to farm the fields, forcing women and children to do the work. The Italian government also had a shortage of soldiers for its army. The positive side of immigration, however, was the money that flowed back to Italy from the Italian Americans. By 1914, the immigrants had sent hundreds of millions of dollars to their families in Italy.

Italian Americans and World War I

During the summer of 1914, World War I erupted in Europe. On one side were the Allies, whose major powers were Great Britain, France, and Russia. They fought against the Central Powers of Germany, Austria-Hungary, and Turkey. Italy fought with the Allies, and as many as 70,000 Italian Americans who were still Italian citizens returned to Europe to fight for their homeland. Lawyer Gino Speranza traveled with some of these Italian Americans as they made the trip back across the Atlantic. He later wrote that some were completely American. They did not speak Italian and wore typical American clothing. "There was even one Italian from Kansas," Speranza noted, "in a baseball suit!"

These Italian Americans joined members of other ethnic groups who left the United States to fight in Europe for the countries of their birth. But the immigrants' loyalty to their homelands raised concern among many U.S. leaders. The immigrants seemed less loyal to their new country and were not truly Americanized. Some important Americans, including carmaker Henry Ford and former president Theodore Roosevelt, wanted to end the immigrants' loyalty to their country of birth. They called for a stronger effort to assimilate the Italians and other immigrants. The new goal for the country was called "100 percent Americanism."

Under 100 percent Americanism, companies and local governments targeted adult immigrants, teaching them English and pushing for their naturalization, or citizenship. Once naturalized in the United States, the immigrants lost their citizenship in the country where they were born. Constantine Panunzio became a U.S. citizen around the time the war began. He had been in the United States 12 years before finally deciding to become naturalized. In his autobiography, he explained the feelings of many immigrants who did not rush to seek U.S. citizenship: "It took no small amount of moral courage to come to the point where I could honestly swear off allegiance from my native country and as honestly turn it to this nation." Panunzio called some of the efforts to Americanize the Italians "cruel," because Americans tried to force the immigrants to forget their native land and their native language. According to Panunzio, Americans said, "Either become an American citizen or get out." But the immigrants, he believed, needed time to make that decision.

When the United States entered the war in 1917, many Italian Americans quickly joined the military. Many were not yet U.S. citizens, and they earned citizenship through their service. They also earned the respect of other Americans. First- and second-generation Italians made up almost 12 percent of the U.S. Army, at a time when Italian Americans were just 4 percent of the country's total population. Ten percent of the U.S soldiers killed during World War I were Italian Americans.

Closing the Door

Despite their loyal service, Italian Americans could not escape discrimination. Many still heard the insulting slang names Americans used for Italians. Nativists were calling for quotas, or limits on the number of immigrants from certain countries allowed to enter the United States. The nativists wanted to promote immigration from Great Britain and northern Europe, and limit immigration from southern and eastern Europe and other parts of the globe.

The efforts to restrict immigration had begun before World War I, when some Americans demanded that immigrants pass a literacy test in order to enter the United States. The government finally approved a test in 1917. Immigrants had to show that they could read in any one language. Few people failed the test. The fighting in Europe kept more

An Indirect Attack on Italians

The drive to limit immigration to the United States came while many Americans were fighting for another legal restriction, on the sale and use of alcohol. Prohibition, as this effort was called, became the law of the land in 1920. To Italians, Prohibition was an assault on their lifestyle, since wine was a part of daily life. An old Italian expression said, "A day without wine is like a day without the sun." Adults drank wine at lunch and dinner, and children would sometimes have it mixed with water. Some men even had it at breakfast, mixed with raw egg. They believed this drink would give them energy. Many Italians made their own wines from grapes they had grown. Prohibition allowed families to produce some wine for their own use, but large Italian wineries suffered, and Italians could not share a bottle of wine in public.

Italians and other immigrants from entering the United States than the literacy test did. But the test indicated the willingness of the United States to restrict immigration.

Laws that set quotas for immigration were passed in 1921 and 1924. Under the 1924 law, the number of immigrants from a European country was limited to 2 percent of that nationality's U.S. population in 1890. In 1890, the Italian-born population in the United States was just under 180,000. Under the new quota system, fewer than 3,600 Italians would be allowed into the country each year (3,600 is 2 percent of 180,000). (The law, however, did make exceptions for certain well-educated Italian immigrants, such as college professors and religious officials.) This quota dramatically restricted Italian immigration, which had been at about 110,000 immigrants per year in the decade from 1911 to 1920.

The quotas reflected the prejudice and fear of many Americans. Some nativists wrongly believed that Italians and other immigrants created most of the problems in the United States, such as crime. The nativists associated immigrants with strikes and other labor problems.

Many Italian Americans and other immigrants protested the quotas. In 1924, a group of Italian-American business owners wrote, "there is nothing that the Americans of Italian birth and extraction have done in this continent that would justify such unfair and brutally cruel treatment." Still, the quota system remained. Fewer birds of passage traveled back and forth between the United States and Italy. Italian neighborhoods would not receive as many new arrivals with fresh memories of the homeland. The Italians who had already settled in the United States worked to save their ethnic heritage while also becoming truly American.

Opposite: A little girl stands in the doorway of an Italian grocery store displaying meats and cheeses in New York City around 1890.

Chapter Four

Becoming American

Assimilation and Prejudice

Adjusting to America

Through the 1920s and 1930s, Italian immigration to the United States continued, although it was greatly reduced by the quotas set in 1924. Far fewer immigrants arrived during this time than in the previous decades.

The Italians who did come followed the old patterns set by the great wave of immigrants before them. The new arrivals went to cities that already had Italian communities, such as New York, Boston, and Chicago. They wanted to be with relatives or friends who had come from the same villages of Italy.

During the 1930s, many Italian Americans returned to Italy. The United States was in the middle of the Great Depression. The economy had weakened and millions of Americans had lost their jobs. Families struggled to pay for food and housing. Many Italians thought they might have a better chance of finding work in Italy. If not, at least they could be with relatives or live in a familiar land, instead of suffering in a foreign country.

Italian Immigration to America

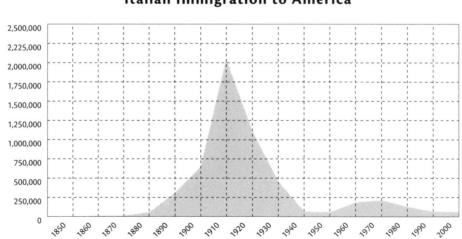

Italian Americans continued to adjust to life in the United States. Although hardworking, most did not move into skilled professions. The Italians did not remain ditchdiggers and ragpickers, but they did not produce many doctors and lawyers. In general, Italian families sent fewer children to college than other ethnic groups did, and girls were less likely to attend than boys. Still, more and more Italian children did stay in school long enough to earn high school degrees, enabling them to improve their family's finances. Many Italians stayed in such fields as construction, farming, and the grocery business. Others took jobs as office workers, teachers, and skilled tradespeople such as plumbers and electricians.

Some Italian Americans pursued careers that brought them and their ethnic group wider public attention. Fiorello La Guardia, for example, was the most famous Italian-American politician of the era. A product of New York's Lower East Side, he served in Congress and was mayor of New York City for 11 years. Italian-American athletes also emerged on the national scene. College basketball star Hank Luisetti won fame during the 1930s. In baseball, Joe DiMaggio joined the New York Yankees in 1936 and became one of the game's greatest players ever. In 1941, DiMaggio hit in 56 consecutive games, a record that still stands today.

Italian Entertainers

During the 1920s and 1930s, several Italian entertainers also emerged as national stars. The radio and motion picture industries grew tremendously during those years, and Italian-American singers and actors won success by drawing on their culture's rich artistic tradition. In the era of silent films, Italian-American actor Rudolph Valentino became one of the first major film stars. The good-looking Valentino was born in Italy and came to the United States in 1913. Known as a "Latin lover," he was especially popular with women. Valentino died in 1926 at age 31, several years before the talkies, or films with sound, became common. A few years later, Domenic Amici changed his name to Don Ameche and became a film star. He was most famous for his role as Alexander Graham Bell, the man given credit for inventing the telephone. Italian American Jimmy Durante, who acted on both stage and in films, was famous for his raspy voice and big nose. His nose earned him the nickname "the Schnozzola" (*schnozzle* is a slang word for "nose").

Luisetti's Famous Shot

Today's typical basketball fan has probably never heard of Angelo "Hank" Luisetti. But basketball experts know that Luisetti greatly influenced the game. During the 1930s, most players shot with two hands and with their feet firmly planted on the floor. While playing for Stanford University, Luisetti perfected a one-handed running shot. During that era, few players scored many points in a game. Luisetti amazed fans when he used his unusual new shot to score 50 points in one Stanford contest. In 1951, Luisetti was named the second-greatest basketball player in the United States from 1900 to 1950. In 1959 Luisetti was one of the first players chosen for the Basketball Hall of Fame.

Italy's traditional role as a center for opera, as well as the popularity of folk songs, made singing an important part of Italian-American culture. Some Italian-American singing stars emerged during the 1930s, though most of these had their greatest success in the decades to come. These singers included Perry Como, Frankie Laine, and Frank Sinatra.

The Negative Side

Some film and music stars intentionally hid their Italian background from American audiences. Frankie Laine, for example, changed his name from LoVecchio. Although most Italian Americans were assimilating and some achieved great success, they still faced prejudice. Events of the 1920s and 1930s had further stirred the country's anti-Italian feelings.

For example, starting in 1920, Prohibition created a new business called bootlegging, which was the selling of illegal liquor. Bootleggers brought in alcohol from Canada or other foreign nations, then sold it at a high profit. Italian-American crime gangs took part in this business, as did Irish, Jewish, and other ethnic gangsters. The Italians, however, already had a bad reputation because of their association with the Mafia, an organized crime group. Furthermore, several of the most well-known gangsters of the era were Italian Americans. In the media, they represented the lawlessness linked to Prohibition.

The most famous U.S. criminal during the 1920s was Al "Scarface" Capone of Chicago. Capone rose to become the most powerful crime boss in Chicago and one of the richest men in America. Along with bootlegging, Capone made his fortune promoting illegal gambling. Writing in 1931, historian Frederick Lewis Allen described the lavish wedding Capone threw for his sister, the estate he owned in Chicago, and a fortune worth perhaps $20 million (nearly $240 million in today's money). "He rode about Chicago in an armored car," Allen wrote, "with another car to patrol the way ahead and a third car full of his armed henchmen [guards] following behind." The U.S. government finally sent Capone to prison in 1931 for not paying his taxes.

Another Italian American soon emerged as a leading crime figure. Charles "Lucky" Luciano, based in New York, is considered the founder of the modern Mafia in America. He made it a national organization run like a business, but one that used violence when necessary to reach its goals. Like Capone, Luciano also ended up in jail.

Capone and Luciano were genuine criminals, violent men who would do almost anything, including commit murder, to get what they wanted. But two Italian Americans who were executed for supposedly breaking the law may not have been criminals at all. The trial of Nicola Sacco and Bartolomeo Vanzetti filled the newspapers during the 1920s, and it remains one of the most famous legal cases in U.S. history.

In April 1920, a group of robbers in Braintree, Massachusetts, killed two men while stealing $16,000. Sacco and Vanzetti were charged with the crime, though both immigrants insisted that they were innocent. Public opinion turned against them because they were anarchists, which means that they believed in complete freedom for individuals and rejected traditional governments. Sacco and Vanzetti had opposed World War I and fled to Mexico rather than serve in the U.S. military. After the war, U.S. and local officials often arrested suspected radicals such as anarchists, fearing they would carry out terrorism to promote their views. This period in U.S. history is known as the Red Scare, because the color red was associated with radicals and Communists.

During the trial of Sacco and Vanzetti in 1921, the government presented weak evidence against the pair. Still, the two men were found guilty, and the judge refused to hear new evidence that might have proven their innocence. The judge also rejected another man's claim that he had taken part in the murders and that Sacco and Vanzetti had not.

Italian-born anarchists and convicted murderers Bartolomeo Vanzetti (center) and Nicola Sacco (right) sit handcuffed to a guard in Dedham, Massachusetts in 1917. They were executed in Boston ten years later.

Most Anglo Americans believed that Sacco and Vanzetti were guilty. Their radical political beliefs were unpopular. Their Italian background also made them suspect. A few people, however, did try to help Sacco and Vanzetti, speaking out against the unfair trial they received. One of these supporters was Felix Frankfurter, a law professor and future justice of the U.S. Supreme Court. In a long magazine article, he pointed out the errors in the trial and listed evidence that supported Sacco and Vanzetti's innocence.

Frankfurter wrote, "The past character and record of Sacco and Vanzetti have always made it . . . incredible that they should spontaneously become perpetrators of a bold murder, executed with the utmost expertness." Despite increasing calls for a new trial, the two men were executed in 1927. Since then, some historians have claimed that both men, or at least Vanzetti, were innocent, while others have said they were guilty as charged.

On April 9, 1927, Bartolomeo Vanzetti made a last statement in court declaring his innocence. He said, in part:

> *This is what I say: I would not wish to a dog or to a snake, to the most low and misfortunate creature of the earth–I would not wish any of them what I have had to suffer for things that I am not guilty of. . . . I am suffering because I am a radical and indeed I am a radical; I have suffered because I was an Italian, and indeed I am an Italian. . . . I am so convinced to be right that if you could execute me two times, and if I could be reborn two other times, I would live again to do what I have done already.*

The Rise of Fascism

During the 1920s and 1930s, changes in Italy's government drew the attention of Italian Americans. In 1922, Benito Mussolini and the Fascist Party came to power. Mussolini ruled as a dictator. He denied political and personal freedoms such as free speech, and he eventually eliminated all other political parties except for the Fascists. Mussolini wanted to restore the honor of the past, when ancient Rome built its empire. Known as *Il Duce* ("the leader"), Mussolini invaded several African nations and turned them into colonies of Italy.

Mussolini also paid attention to the millions of Italians living in the United States. In some cities, he funded schools that taught the Italian language to young second-generation Italian Americans. Many Italian Americans, as well as Anglo Americans, spoke well of Mussolini and the stronger Italy he was trying to build. Writing about this era in 1942, Italian-American scholar Max Ascoli said that Italian Americans "were proud to see how the most important Americans— bankers, university presidents, writers—were paying tribute to [Mussolini]."

Some Italian Americans, however, saw that Mussolini's fascism was a threat to democracy and liberty. Many Italian Americans spoke out against Mussolini. The antifascist efforts received a boost from Italians who left Italy to escape fascism. These people, known as exiles, included political leaders, artists, writers, educators, and priests. The United States offered them the freedom that Mussolini denied his people in Italy.

Wartime Helper

One of the most important Italian immigrants to reach the United States during the fascist era was scientist Enrico Fermi. Married to a Jewish woman, Fermi took his family out of Italy as Mussolini began imitating German dictator Hitler and placing harsh legal restrictions on Jews. After receiving the highest honor in science, the Nobel Prize, Fermi arrived in New York in 1939. He was studying radiation, a form of energy found in most things on earth. Some metals contain large amounts of radiation, and during the war Fermi explored how to take that energy and use it in a bomb. Fermi's work led to the development of the first nuclear weapon. The United States dropped two of these powerful bombs on Japan in August 1945, helping to end the war. Fermi became a U.S. citizen in 1944. After the war, Congress gave him the Congressional Medal of Merit, the highest honor it can give to a civilian.

Some of the Italians who opposed fascism and came to America had brilliant careers. Unlike the typical Italian immigrants of the previous decades, they were well educated. Max Ascoli, for example, had studied law before emigrating in 1931. In the United States, he worked at several universities and wrote often about Italian Americans. He noted that some of the Italian exiles of the time hoped to return to Italy when Mussolini was no longer in power. Others planned to remain in the United States and become Americans.

Other notable exiles were Arturo Toscanini, an orchestra conductor; diplomat Carlo Sforza; and Giuseppe Borgese, an author.

Italian Americans and World War II

In 1936, Mussolini and Germany's Adolf Hitler signed an agreement that united their two countries in what was called the Rome-Berlin Axis. Mussolini and Hitler later signed a treaty with Japan, creating what were called the Axis Powers. In 1939, Germany began World War II (1939–1945) with a surprise attack on Poland. Japan, meanwhile, was already fighting for control of large parts of China.

On the whole, Italian Americans did not like Mussolini's alliance with Hitler. And when Italy entered World War II in 1940, Italian Americans did not rush to fight for Italy, as they had in World War I. Instead, they remained loyal to the United

It's a Fact

The exact figure is not known, but between 500,000 and 1 million Italian Americans fought for the United States during World War II.

States. Tens of thousands proved their loyalty after December 7, 1941, when a surprise attack by Japan on an American naval base at Pearl Harbor, Hawaii, drew the United States into the war. A recently naturalized Italian American summed up the feeling of many members of his ethnic group. Shortly after the Pearl Harbor attack, he wrote, "I am proud to be [an American] and I shall help in every possible way to keep America on top of the world."

Italian Americans in New York City celebrate the surrender of Japan, which ended World War II in August 1945. With Italy fighting against the United States, the war marked a difficult time for Italian Americans.

Soon after the Japanese attack, the United States declared war on Italy and Germany. Italian Americans who were not U.S. citizens were classified as enemy aliens. At the time, the Italian-American community had more nonnaturalized residents (600,000) than any other ethnic group in the country. Government officials worried that some of these aliens would be loyal to Italy and try to hurt the U.S. war effort. President Franklin Roosevelt ordered the arrest of several hundred Italians who seemed to pose the biggest threat to security. Italian and German aliens, however, did not face the harsh treatment that Japanese Americans did. In the case of the Japanese, both aliens and U.S. citizens were forced out of their homes and into prison-like camps for the entire war.

Enemy alien laws placed some restrictions on Italians. They could not travel far from their homes or be on the street at night. Some were refused jobs in factories that supplied the military with equipment and weapons. And a few Italians were forced out of their homes, just as the Japanese were. Most of the restrictions, however, ended in October 1942. The rest ended the following year, when Italian leaders forced Mussolini from power and joined America's side in the war. By this time, Italian Americans had proven their loyalty to the United States. Young Italian-American men joined the military and Italian-American women of all ages worked in factories producing supplies and equipment for the war. These efforts lessened the prejudice against Italian Americans and helped their assimilation into the broader U.S. culture. 🏵

Opposite: Singer Concetta Fraconero, who used the more "American"-sounding name Connie Francis, was just one of the many Italian Americans who emerged in mainstream American popular culture in the decades after World War II.

Chapter Five

Smaller Numbers, Larger Influence

*Italian Americans
after World War II*

Life in Italy Improves

World War II devastated large areas of Europe, including Italy. Thousands of miles of railroad, as well as tunnels, bridges, homes, and businesses, were destroyed. The United States helped rebuild Italy and other European nations with an aid program called the Marshall Plan. The plan provided money and equipment to repair the damage caused by the war. The U.S. government also passed laws that made it easier for Europeans to emigrate to the United States. Italian immigration increased during the 1950s; more than 180,000 immigrants arrived between 1951 and 1960, the highest number since the 1920s.

Hestor Street in the Little Italy section of New York City was typical of the urban neighborhoods in which many Italian immigrants lived in the 1940s and 1950s.

As Italy's economy improved, people did not need to leave the country to find work. Instead, immigrants tended to come to the United States to join relatives or because they were highly skilled. A new immigration law passed in 1965 ended the old quota system, allowing more southern Europeans, including Italians, into the United States. While the number of Italians entering the country began to rise, it never passed 30,000 per year. From 1971 to 1980, an average of 13,000 Italians arrived in the United States each year. For the next 10 years, the average fell to just a little more than 3,000 per year.

The new arrivals tended to settle in established Italian-American communities. At times, however, the new immigrants felt that Italian Americans did not welcome them. Maria Manzone arrived in Brooklyn during the 1970s. She told two professors studying immigrants, "You'd think the Italians who've been here would try to help us. But they keep saying that we have it too good. Too good because we didn't find the prejudice and hard times that their grandparents found."

Assimilation Continues

For second- and third-generation Italian Americans, the years following World War II brought major changes. The U.S. government set up a program called the G.I. Bill to help returning soldiers. The program helped them pay for a college education or purchase a home. Through this program, more Italian Americans went to college, though still in smaller numbers than members of other ethnic groups. Many Italians, especially men, were content to work in professions that paid well but did not require a college education, such as construction or the food industry. Many also preferred the satisfaction of owning their own business instead of working for a large company.

One successful business owner was Patsy D'Agostino. He had arrived in the United States in 1920. When he first came to New York, D'Agostino wrote, he and his father "ended up behind pushcarts on the streets of Harlem. . . . It was no place to make a fast dollar." Through hard work, D'Agostino went from his pushcart (a wheeled cart holding merchandise for sale that could be pushed through the streets) to owning a large grocery business that made him a millionaire and that still exists today. By 1952, he was the head of the National Association of Retail Grocers.

Italian Americans such as D'Agostino joined the members of other ethnic groups who left large cities to live in new suburbs. Italians also began to marry outside their ethnic group, but they still remained loyal to many of their old customs. *Feste* and holiday celebrations helped Italian Americans maintain their ties to the "old country," even as they became more Americanized.

The continuing assimilation process led to more Italian Americans taking on important roles in business. Jeno Paulucci, for example, founded several companies that sold frozen foods. In 1949, Candido Jacuzzi invented a pump that he used to create the first hot tubs. To some people today, all tubs with swirling warm water are known as Jacuzzis, even the ones not built by Jacuzzi's company. The same thing happened with Frank Zamboni's invention. Zamboni created a machine that would quickly apply a new layer of ice to skating rinks. Americans began to call any machine that prepared ice for skating a Zamboni.

In the 1960s and 1970s, a number of Italian Americans rose to top positions in the auto industry. John Riccardo served as the head of Chrysler, and Lee Iacocca headed both that company and Ford.

Mustang Man

During the 1980s, Lido "Lee" Iacocca made headlines as the head of Chrysler. The automaker almost collapsed before Iacocca convinced the U.S. government to help the company borrow $1.5 billion. Iacocca's programs at Chrysler were a success, and the company paid back the loans years before they were due. Iacocca had already won fame years earlier for his work at Ford. He led the committee that designed and sold the Mustang, a sporty, inexpensive car that appealed to young people. The Mustang forced other car companies to build similar cars. Today, the Mustang remains one of the most popular U.S. cars ever built.

Political Success

In politics, Italian Americans began to rise to national prominence during the 1950s and 1960s. John Pastore served as governor of Rhode Island before becoming the first Italian-American senator, winning his first term in 1950. He remained in the U.S. Senate until 1976. John Volpe of Massachusetts was governor of his state before becoming the first Italian to serve in a president's cabinet (the advisers in charge of the most important government agencies). In 1969, President Richard Nixon named Volpe secretary of transportation. Later notable Italian-American politicians included Mario Cuomo, governor of New York from 1982 through 1994; Alfonse D'Amato, a U.S. senator from New York State from 1981 through 1998; and Leon Panetta, a member of the U.S. House of Representatives who later served as a key aide to President Bill Clinton.

Italian-American women also began appearing in politics. Ella Tambussi Grasso of Connecticut was the first American woman of any nationality to become governor of a state on her

A Top Judge

In 1986, President Ronald Reagan named Antonin Scalia to the U.S. Supreme Court, the most powerful court in the country. Scalia was the first Italian American to reach the Supreme Court. Scalia, a second-generation Italian American, completed his law degree in 1960. He taught at several colleges and held government jobs under Presidents Richard Nixon and Gerald Ford. In 1982, Reagan gave Scalia his first judgeship, naming him to a federal court.

On the Supreme Court, Scalia is known for his sharp intellect and fine writing skills. He is also the Court's most conservative judge. Scalia believes that the Supreme Court should closely follow what is written in the U.S. Constitution and not try to create new policies.

own, without ties to a politically important husband. Grasso governed Connecticut from 1975 through 1980. She had earlier served in Congress. In 1984, Geraldine Ferraro made history as the first American woman to run for the vice presidency for a major political party. Another Italian-American woman to make political history was Nancy Pelosi. In 2002, Democrats in the House of Representatives elected her to lead the party in the House. Pelosi was the first woman to lead a major party in either branch of Congress.

Except for Volpe and D'Amato, all of these prominent Italian-American politicians were Democrats. Italians tended to vote Democratic through the 1970s. But since that time, more Italians have begun to join the Republican Party or at least vote for Republican candidates, just as they had done a century before. In 1979, for example, the vast majority of Italian Americans in Congress were Democrats. During the 1990s, the number of Italian-American lawmakers in Congress was almost evenly split between the two major parties. Some political experts suggest that economics played a role in this change. As Italians became successful and made more money, they favored Republican policies, such as cutting taxes.

Achievements in the Arts

In the decades after World War II, Italian Americans made great contributions to both popular culture and more serious art forms, such as literature and painting. Frank Sinatra continued his wartime popularity, and he was joined by other singers such as Dean Martin (Dino Paul Crocetti) and Tony Bennett (Anthony Benedetto). Sinatra and Martin also pursued acting careers, and Sinatra and Bennett reached new audiences during the 1990s when they recorded songs with rock stars.

America after World War II experienced a baby boom as returning soldiers married and started families in large numbers. In the 1950s, the growing youth population fueled the growth of rock and roll music. Rock blended several different musical forms, most of them coming out of African-American culture. Italian Americans used their traditional talents for singing and composing to make an impact on rock and other pop music. Bobby Darin (Walden Roberto Cassotto) wrote several top hits during the late 1950s, then began a singing career. Concetta Fraconero, who sang under the name Connie Francis, had a number-one hit in 1957 with "Who's Sorry Now." Other Italian Americans who followed Francis onto the record charts were Frankie Valli (Francis Castelluccio) and Frankie Avalon (Francis Avallone).

In the decades that followed the birth of rock and roll, more Italian Americans sang their way into American homes. Two of these performers made their biggest impact in Broadway musicals. Liza Minnelli is the daughter of Italian-American film director Vincente Minnelli and actress Judy Garland, the star of *The Wizard of Oz*. Like her mother, Liza Minnelli has won success in both singing and acting. So has Bernadette Peters (Bernadette Lazzara), who still performs regularly on Broadway.

Minnelli and Peters joined a long list of Italian Americans who have enjoyed successful careers as actors. Some other notable stars are Alan Alda, featured on the popular TV show *M*A*S*H;* Sylvester Stallone, creator of the *Rocky* film series; John Travolta, who starred in several hit films; and Nicholas Cage (Nichola Coppola), who won an Academy Award, the film industry's highest honor, in 1996. On television, comedian Ray Romano emerged in the early 2000s as a top star.

Sylvester Stallone (left) and John Travolta (right), pictured in 1983, are two of the many Italian-American movie actors who have achieved huge fame and popularity in the entertainment industry.

In motion pictures, the key person behind the camera is the director. Several notable directors of the late 20th and early 21st centuries are Italian Americans. The most famous is Francis Ford Coppola (father of writer and director Sofia Coppola and uncle of actor Nicolas Cage), who directed the three *Godfather* films. Brian De Palma, meanwhile, won fame for his thrillers. One of his most famous movies was *Scarface*, a 1983 remake of a 1932 film about a gangster. (In the original *Scarface*, the lead character was loosely based on real-life gangster Al Capone.) Many films by Italian-American directors explore life in their ethnic communities and issues important to their ethnic group, such as family, religion, and getting along in Anglo culture. Others, such as Coppola's *Godfather* films, explore the association of Italians with organized crime.

In Love with Pizza

Italian-American singer Dean Martin

People in Europe have eaten flatbread covered with toppings for more than 2,000 years. Italian immigrants from Naples introduced the modern pizza to the United States around 1900. The first pizzerias were in Italian communities. Americans in general, however, did not discover pizza until the 1950s. A song recorded in 1953 by Dean Martin supposedly boosted pizza's popularity. He sang, "When the moon hits your eye like a big pizza pie, that's *amore*" (*amore* is the Italian word for "love"). Around that time, an Italian-American business introduced the first frozen pizzas, making it easy for anyone to enjoy them at home.

Art and Writing

Hundreds of years ago, Italian artists shaped the Renaissance, an art movement in the 1500s influenced by the beautiful art of ancient Greece and Rome. After the Renaissance, painting and sculpture remained part of the Italian art tradition. Starting in the early 19th century, several Italian artists came to the United States to create works for public buildings. In the 20th century, Italian Americans continued to play a part in the art world. Clara Fasano was a noted sculptor, and Robert Fasanella painted many scenes of average workers and their daily lives. Joseph Stella is best known for a series of paintings showing New York City. The best-known modern artist of Italian descent is Frank Stella (no relation to Joseph). He has often used geometric shapes and bright colors in his works.

A Special Kind of Art

The Chinese invented fireworks about 1,100 years ago. Italians, however, became experts at making and setting off fireworks for large celebrations. Today, the company known as Fireworks by Grucci is the most famous fireworks maker in the United States. The Grucci family traces its roots to an Italian immigrant who learned how to make fireworks in Italy. He brought his skill to America, and future generations developed the family business. In 1979, the Gruccis became the first Americans to win a gold medal at the world's most important fireworks competition. Since then, Fireworks by Grucci has created colorful displays for many important events, including the Olympic Games, world fairs in the United States and Asia, and the 100th anniversary of the Statue of Liberty.

Cartoons and Comics

Some people may see cartoons and comics as kids' stuff, but many others consider them a true art form. Several Italian Americans played a part in developing the art of cartoon animation. Starting in the early 1940s, Walter Lantz (Lanza) created Woody Woodpecker and several other cartoon characters. Joseph Barbera, with his partner William Hanna, had a long career in animation. Hanna and Barbera created cat-and-mouse team Tom and Jerry, the Flintstones, and Scooby-Doo, among many other characters.

In the world of comic books, some notable artists were Italian Americans. Carmine Infantino, for instance, illustrated books featuring the superheroes Flash and Green Lantern. For a time, John Romita drew Spiderman and other characters for Marvel Comics. Frank Frazetta drew both comic books and comic strips. He won his greatest fame drawing fantasy and science fiction comics for adult audiences. Frazetta's detailed paintings of such characters as Tarzan and Conan the Barbarian have sold thousands of copies.

Along with a rich artistic tradition, Italy has produced some of the world's greatest writers, including Dante Alighieri (1265–1321), author of *The Divine Comedy*. The first Italian-American writers who worked in English often wrote about their immigrant communities or wrote autobiographies (books about their own lives). In the years after World War II, Italian-American writers turned to poetry and fiction to express themselves.

The Beats were a group of poets interested in social and political issues and the influence of Asian cultures. Several important Beat writers were Italian Americans, including Lawrence Ferlinghetti and Gregory Corso. Noted Italian-American novelists include Don DeLillo and Mario Puzo. DeLillo has written on a variety of topics, including a fictional look at Lee Harvey Oswald, the man who assassinated President John F. Kennedy in 1963. Puzo's most famous work is *The Godfather*, about an Italian-American Mafia family. Francis Ford Coppola based his *Godfather* films on this 1969 book. Puzo's work led to a new interest in the Mafia as a subject for books and films.

Exploring the Link to Organized Crime

Puzo's book appeared after Americans had heard new evidence that linked Italian Americans and organized crime. World War II gave many Italians the chance to prove their loyalty to the United States. That loyal service, however, did not end the stereotype of Italians as criminals, especially as members of crime gangs.

A New Generation of Film Gangsters

The first gangster movies appeared during the 1930s, with Italian Americans often the main characters. Decades later, *The Godfather*, released in 1972, led to a new round of gangster films, focused on the Mafia. *The Godfather II* came out in 1974, and the third *Godfather* movie came out in 1990. These movies boosted the careers of Francis Ford Coppola and several Italian-American actors, including Al Pacino and Robert De Niro. *The Godfather* has been called one of the greatest films ever made. The story shows the workings of the Mafia, but it also addresses larger issues, such as family loyalty and how immigrants succeed in the United States.

The Godfather and other Mafia films shaped the popular view of the Mafia in the U.S. media. These films also influenced real gangsters. One law official said that in secretly taped conversations, real criminals began to talk like the Mafia members shown in the movies.

Actor Robert De Niro (second from right, in cap) is pictured in a scene from the movie The Godfather, Part II *in 1974. The movie was directed by Italian American Francis Ford Coppola.*

In 1950, a committee from the U.S. Senate began to study organized crime in several U.S. cities. In 1951, the committee came to New York City. Its hearings were broadcast on TV, and millions of Americans saw Frank Costello, an Italian-American crime figure, nervously answering questions. At one point, Costello left the hearings and was arrested for refusing to cooperate.

The Senate hearings showed that crime gangs controlled gambling and other illegal activities in many cities. Not all these gangs were Italian, but based on weak evidence the Senate stated that the Mafia existed in the United States. The committee's report called the Mafia a "sinister . . . criminal organization" directly connected to "the criminal organization of the same name originating in the Island of Sicily." The hearings and the report added to the image of Italian Americans, especially Sicilians, as dangerous gangsters, reinforcing the stereotype already held by many Americans.

Less than 10 years later, another Senate committee looked into the power and structure of the Mafia. This time the government had a key witness, named Frank Valachi. A convicted criminal and murderer, Valachi claimed that he knew about the Mafia's operations. Valachi described five "families," based in New York, that supposedly controlled other Italian crime groups. A book about Valachi appeared in 1968, and Mario Puzo's novel followed the next year. Soon, most Americans knew about the Mafia families and their operations.

The popularity of *The Godfather* and other Mafia stories influenced many Americans, and today Italian Americans still battle their image as gangsters. Yet a man who helped shape the negative attitudes of many Americans about Italians said he grew up in a household proud of its Italian heritage. Francis Ford Coppola said his father always told him about "the Italian genius and the tremendous achievement in all the great fields." His father, Coppola said, "made a very convincing point to us that we should feel part of a very exalted culture and should in no way feel inferior as Italian Americans." ▩

Opposite: *Two Italian-American girls wear traditional costumes at an Italian festival in Kansas City, Missouri, in 1975.*

Chapter Six

Italian
Americans Today

Ethnic Pride

Today's Immigration

At the start of the 21st century, the number of Italians emigrating to the United States remained at about 3,000 per year. Italy's economy has continued to do well, compared to the years before World War II, so Italians can easily find jobs at home instead of heading to another country to find work. Many of the people who do emigrate choose to stay in Europe rather than come to North America. A new political arrangement among most of the European nations, called the European Union, makes it easier for the citizens of one European country to work and live in another. As during the 1970s and 1980s, most of the Italians who do come to America settle with relatives or take highly skilled jobs.

Most Italian immigrants have settled in these states.

Although the number of new arrivals has sharply decreased, the descendants of earlier Italian immigrants continue to play an important role in the United States. Their ties to their ethnic background are strong, even as their assimilation has increased.

Italian Americans continue to marry people of other ethnic backgrounds, yet many still choose to identify themselves as Italian. Italian Americans are more likely to identify with their ethnic roots than members of other European ethnic groups. And the number of Americans who call themselves Italians continues to rise. In the 2000 census, the number of Americans who said they were Italian increased by 1 million over the 1990 census. This was far more than the number of new Italian immigrants who settled in the country during that decade. This response suggests that Americans of Italian descent are increasingly proud to proclaim their ethnic background.

The 2000 census showed that almost 16 million Americans had Italian roots and considered themselves Italian Americans. They were the fourth-largest European ethnic group in the country, after the Irish, English, and German. About another 10 million Americans have ethnic ties to Italy but do not call themselves Italian Americans.

The census also showed how well the later generations of Italian Americans had done economically, compared to the millions who came to the United States during the late 19th and early 20th centuries. By 2000, almost one in five Italian Americans had earned a college degree, slightly higher than the figure for all Americans combined, and the average income for these Italian Americans was more than $61,000. That figure was more than $10,000 higher than the average salary for all Americans. Two out of three Italian Americans held a white-collar job, which usually requires a college degree or some kind of education beyond high school. White-collar jobs are usually done in offices, as opposed to blue-collar jobs, which are often performed in factories or at construction sites. Until recently, most Italian Americans had blue-collar jobs, since many of them could not afford to go to college or preferred working outside of offices.

Italian Americans Everywhere

Some traits of the Italian immigrants of the late 19th and early 20th century remain the same today for Italian Americans, both recent immigrants and descendants of the earlier immigrants. More live in New York and surrounding states than in any other part of the country, though California has the third-largest Italian population of all the states. Florida has also seen an increase in the number of its Italian-American residents. This might be connected to the large number of people from the Northeast who move to Florida when they retire. New York City, with almost 700,000 Italian Americans, has more than four times as many Italians as Philadelphia and other cities with large Italian populations.

Throughout their time in the United States, Italians have tried to preserve parts of their culture. The religious *feste* of the past are still important, along with other festivals that celebrate Italian heritage. In 2003, more than 300 Italian festivals took place across the country, most of them in the Northeast. Some celebrations are tied to Columbus Day. Many Italians see Christopher Columbus as a national hero and honor his role in linking Europe and North America more than 500 years ago. The first Columbus Day celebration took place in New York in 1792. In 1971, the U.S. government made Columbus Day a federal holiday, to be celebrated on the second Monday in October each year.

Italian-American men play in a boccie tournament in New York City in 1996. Boccie is a popular game in Italian-American communities across the United States.

Despite their acculturation and assimilation, Italian Americans still look back to their homeland. Most do not send money back to Italy or return there to retire, but many still have relatives there, even if only distant cousins. Some Italian Americans travel to the small villages or city neighborhoods where their grandparents or great-grandparents were born. Italians in Italy also have an interest in the United States. The whole world watches American movies and listens to American music, but Italians have a special interest in the Italian Americans who succeed in those fields and others.

Visiting the Homeland

Annamarie DiBartolo Haught is a lawyer in Connecticut. Her mother was born in Sicily and her father is a second-generation Italian American. On visits to Sicily between 1978 and 1994, Haught found sentimental ties to the land of her ancestors. "You walk around and people tell you, 'This is the church where your grandmother and great-grandmother got married. This is the town square, and . . . your mother played here.'" In the United States, Haught was surrounded by relatives who spoke Sicilian and practiced the old customs. In Sicily, she says, "I didn't feel like a tourist. It felt very comfortable."

Today Sicily is not as poor as it once was, and American films, music, and television have introduced American culture to Sicilians who have never set foot in the United States. Haught believes that many Sicilians still look up to the immigrants who crossed the Atlantic and still see the United States as "a great place to come and make your way."

The Italian Inside

Journalist Gay Talese has written on many subjects, including his Italian heritage. In an interview, Talese tried to explain how he feels about being both Italian and American: "There is an Italian inside of me; he talks to me, tells me things, reminds me of others. But I do not understand him; I do not speak his language. I am an American, but an incomplete American: I miss that part (mine or my family's . . .), which remained in Italy or inside my father."

The Continuing Battle

With all their success in the United States, Italian Americans still face prejudice from many other Americans. Some of the prejudice is linked to the lasting image of Italians as gangsters. The TV show *The Sopranos,* which began in 1999, portrays a modern Italian-American family associated with the Mafia. Tony Soprano, the main character, and his wife, Carmela, face many of the same problems all Americans face, such as rebellious children and difficulties with their marriage. The show has touches of humor and deep emotion. Yet *The Sopranos* also contributes to the image of Italians as criminals. Italian Americans also face the stereotype that they are not well educated and take mostly blue-collar jobs. Television shows and movies rarely show Italians as business owners or bankers.

In 2003, the Order Sons of Italy in America released the results of two surveys. They showed that 78 percent of U.S. teens associated Italians with

It's a Fact!

According to U.S. government figures, less than .0025 percent of Italian Americans are involved in organized crime.

blue-collar jobs or the Mafia. Almost the same number of adults held a similar view. A spokesperson from the OSIA said, "There's a long tradition of stereotyping Italian Americans as violent gangsters or lovable losers. We'd like to see these [images] buried."

Italian American Rudolph Giuliani was the mayor of New York City at the time of the terrorist attacks of September 11, 2001. He was photographed during a ceremony to mark the three-month anniversary of the attacks.

The continuing contributions of Italian Americans to American society will help end the prejudice and stereotypes. One person who has played a key role in this process is

Rudolph Giuliani. During the 1980s, Giuliani, working as an attorney, led the fight against organized crime members and other powerful criminals in New York. In 1993, he was elected mayor of New York City. As mayor, he reduced crime and made the city more attractive to visitors. "Rudy," as he was known, won his greatest respect in the face of disaster. He was still the mayor of New York City on September 11, 2001, when terrorists flew two planes into the Twin Towers of the World Trade Center. With the buildings destroyed and almost 3,000 people dead, Giuliani took charge during the emergency. Most important, during the city's worst crisis, he offered New Yorkers hope for better times.

Giuliani served the city as a proud New Yorker. He also showed how millions of Italian immigrants have left behind the idea of *campanilismo*, or loyalty to only their own ethnic community. Family and the local community are still important to Italians in the United States, but so is being an American. Italian Americans will continue to balance their ties to their old culture with their love for their new homeland. 🏵

Time Line of Italian Immigration

1492	Searching for a route to Asia, Christopher Columbus reaches North America.
1524	Giovanni da Verrazano is the first European to explore what is now New York Harbor.
1678	Working for France, Enrico di Tonti explores the Mississippi River.
1773	Philip Mazzei lands in Virginia and soon takes an active role in promoting American independence from Great Britain.
1851–1860	More than 9,000 Italian immigrants arrive in the United States.
1870	The modern nation of Italy is born, dominated by politicians from the north.
1880	A great wave of Italian immigration begins, sending millions of people to the United States.
1885	Congress passes a law to end the padrone system.
1886	Francis Spinola of New York is the first Italian American elected to the U.S. House of Representatives.
1889	Italian nun Frances Cabrini arrives in New York; she later becomes the first U.S. citizen named a saint in the Roman Catholic Church.
1892	Ellis Island opens, the first stop in the United States for millions of Italians.
1901–1910	Italian immigration to the United States reaches its peak, as more than 2 million Italians enter the country.
1904	Amadeo Giannini opens Banca d'Italia in San Francisco; it later becomes Bank of America, one of the largest banks in the country.
1905	Order Sons of Italy in America (OSIA) is founded to help Italian immigrants adjust to life in the United States.
1912	Italian-American labor leaders play a key role during a strike in Lawrence, Massachusetts.

1917–1918	Italian Americans prove their loyalty as they fight for the United States during World War I.
1922	Benito Mussolini takes over as the political leader of Italy.
1924	Congress sets up a quota system that sharply reduces the number of Italian immigrants allowed into the United States.
1927	Nicola Sacco and Bartolomeo Vanzetti are executed for murder, though both men claim they are innocent.
1934	Fiorello La Guardia is elected mayor of New York City.
1950	John Pastore of Rhode Island becomes the first Italian American elected to the U.S. Senate.
1951	The U.S. Senate investigates Italian Americans involved in organized crime and promotes the idea of the Mafia as a major crime group.
1965	Congress ends the old quota system for immigration, but overall the number of Italians settling in the United States remains low.
1969	John Volpe, appointed secretary of transportation under President Richard Nixon, becomes the first Italian-American member of a president's cabinet.
1972	Francis Ford Coppola releases *The Godfather*, which wins many awards but reinforces the stereotype that Italian Americans are associated with organized crime.
1984	Geraldine Ferraro is the first woman to run for U.S. vice president on a major party ticket.
1986	Antonin Scalia becomes the first Italian American to serve on the U.S. Supreme Court.
2001	Rudolph Giuliani, mayor of New York City, becomes a national hero for his leadership after the September 11 terrorist attacks on the World Trade Center.
2002	Italian-American congresswoman Nancy Pelosi of California is the first woman to lead a major political party in Congress.
2003	Order Sons of Italy in America releases a survey showing that many Americans associate Italians with the Mafia as a result of media stereotypes.

Glossary

assimilate Absorb or blend into the way of life of a society.

culture The language, arts, traditions, and beliefs of a society.

democracy Government by the majority rule of the people.

emigrate Leave one's homeland to live in another country.

ethnic Having certain racial, national, tribal, religious, or cultural origins.

fascist Person with extremely conservative political beliefs, favoring a strong military and limits on political freedoms for nonfascists.

festa Italian festival to honor a saint, another important person, or a special event.

immigrate Come to a foreign country to live.

mutual aid society Group formed by immigrants to help new arrivals who face social or economic difficulties.

padrone Italian for "boss"; person who paid for immigrants to come to America and found them jobs in return for part of the immigrants' pay.

prejudice Negative opinion formed without just cause.

quota A certain percentage of a total number; a share.

refugee Someone who flees a place for safety reasons, especially to another country.

stereotype Simplified and sometimes insulting opinion or image of a person or group.

tenement Type of crowded apartment building designed to house as many people as possible, often in unhealthy conditions.

Further Reading

BOOKS

Aldridge, Rebecca. *Italian Americans*. Philadelphia: Chelsea House, 2003.

Monroe, Judy. *The Sacco and Vanzetti Controversial Murder Trial: A Headline Court Case*. Berkeley Heights, N.J.: Enslow, 2000.

Morreale, Ben, and Robert Carola. *Italian Americans: The Immigrant Experience*. Westport, Conn.: Hugh Lauter Levin Associates, 2000.

Murphy, Jim. *Pick and Shovel Poet: The Journeys of Pascal D'Angelo*. New York: Clarion, 2000.

Petrini, Catherine M. *The Italian Americans*. San Diego: Lucent, 2002.

Weinberger, Kimberly. *Journey to a New Land: An Oral History*. New York: Mondo, 2000.

WEB SITES

Fireworks by Grucci—Since 1850. "Announcing the 2004 Summer Fireworks Season!" URL: http://www.grucci.com. Updated on June 21, 2004.

Italian American Museum. "Home Page." URL: http://www.italian americanmuseum.org/. Downloaded on June 24, 2004.

Italian Food Forever. "Welcome." URL: http://www.italianfood forever.com/. Downloaded on June 24, 2004.

Order Sons of Italy in America (OSIA). "One Stop Italian America: Your passport to the very best of Italian America." URL: http://www.osia.org/. Downloaded on June 24, 2004.

Index

Page numbers in *italics* indicate photographs. Page numbers followed by *m* indicate maps. Page numbers followed by *g* indicate glossary entries. Page numbers in **boldface** indicate box features.